ALIVE

ALIVE

Spring to Life

DR. M. DAVID CHAMBERS

DDC 4 Him Productions

~ 1 ~

"MIDNIGHT CRY"

"There's been an accident." The Doctors words were heavy and cold. This simple statement evoked so many thoughts and emotions all at once in the Father's heart and mind who held the phone awaiting more details with bated breath. None came. Realizing the Physician was allowing him time to process, Thomas finally snapped out of his shock-induced stupor and in rapid fire questioning, "What do you mean, what happened, who was involved, what's going on?!" "It's your son, Dairs, Mr. Clayton." The Doctor went on to explain that he was the resident Neurologist at Bladen County

Hospital, Dr. Davis, and was attending to Thomas's teenage son. "He was involved in an accident on the lake today and sustained a major head injury, and I have to be honest the situation is dire." The Father slumped against the wall and became sick to his stomach. Beyond the fog brought on by the shock of it all, he was able to mutter, "tell me what happened, what's happening and what should I do, is there anyone with him?" "Apparently they were playing a game called "King of the Pier," the specialist replied, "and in the process he was accidentally shoved head-first into a broken pier piling sticking up out of the water. The force caused your son to sustain a severe skull fracture and there is significant swelling on the brain. If we cannot stop the swelling there will be brain damage, or possibly even death. We have sent everyone out of the room so we can properly care for him, but his friend Dolian refuses to leave his side, so he is not alone. If you can, you need to get here as soon as you are able." "Save my son, please sir, save my son", the broken parent retorted. "We will do everything we can sir," and at that the phone went dead.

The distraught Father dropped the phone and fell to his knees by his bedside and immediately began crying out. "Please God, please heal my son, take me and anything I have, but please don't take my boy-he's only 16 with his whole life ahead of him, please Lord save him and I will dedicate him totally to you and do all I can to point him to you." After making a couple of calls to get the boy's Grandmother, and others praying, Thomas grabbed a couple of things and jumped in the car with his bride, Kaye. They drove into the darkness of night, praying the entire way at breakneck speed, turning the otherwise 3-hour trip into just barely a 2-hour sprint. So focused on getting to his son, the forlorn Dad watched as the winding ribbon of road with it's yellow and white stripes became one continuous blur. In this time before cell phones, the couple knew nothing beyond what the doctor had shared before leaving home, and were starving for more answers, and it seemed they could not get there quickly enough. Finally arriving at the hospital, the distressed parents nearly fell out of the car and ran into the hospital...

~ 2 ~

"BOYS WILL BE BOYS"

The Day before...

"Come on boys, load up or get left behind!" The Youth leader was already flustered after wrangling the bakers dozen of teen boys several times in an attempt to get the bus loaded to head out on their White Lake Camp Adventure. The bus ride was grueling in "Old Bertha" as the beaten-up old school bus, now turned church bus, was affectionately known. Thirteen boys, 3 chaperones and no air conditioning on one old bus made for some interesting travels, not to mention the smells and sounds that seemed to just follow this wild bunch of country boys. The trip was to be about 3 hours, but would prove to be more like 4 ½ with all the "necessary" bathroom breaks (which were really only an excuse to stop at a convenience store and waste some of the money given to the kids by their parents on snacks and treats to help keep the local dentists in business). Finally arriving around lunchtime, the chaperones quickly unloaded the bus, directed the kids to their rooms in the cabin and began to make sandwiches for lunch. After scarfing down more cold cuts and cheese than should be allowed by law in record time, the boys bounded out of the cabin towards the lake, with an already exhausted chaperone trailing behind.

The afternoon was spent in grand fashion; treasure dives (with rocks, sticks, and any other item that would sink to the bottom of the crystal-clear waters of the lake), fierce games of chicken (fit for the Summer Olympics), dodgeball (using beach balls until they were utterly destroyed), and showing off for the girls at the pier next door were all a part of the perfect Summer day's activities. Before anyone realized, hours had passed and it was time for devotions and supper.

The group would do devotions first, then eat, because the chaperones knew in their wisdom that getting 13 boys to sit still and listen without something to "motivate" (bribe) them with was futile. Kirby, the Youth Leader, yelled out over the ruckus, "If you guys will sit and pay attention to the lesson, we will have supper and then you can go swimming for a little while longer." At this, the boys snapped to attention except Scott, who quipped, "I thought you had to wait an hour after eating to swim?" "That's ridiculous", said the frazzled leader, "now sit down and pay attention." The lesson was derived from the Biblical account of the Good Samaritan about making your life count for something special by always being on the lookout for opportunities to help others. After some questions, discussion and a closing prayer, the short attention spans turned to the promised dinner of choice for teens the world over- pizza. If ever pizza has been devoured quicker it has not been recorded, it is regretful that *The Guinness Book Of World Records* was not on site to witness and chronicle the speed at which 30 large pizzas, 3 bags of chips, and 7 two-liter sodas disappeared. It was even said that the meal was consumed so fast that two pizza boxes went missing without anyone knowing where to (if you ask any of the boys on the trip, they will tell you to this day, the chaperones ate them because the pizza disappeared so fast). Before the last crumb could be completely swallowed, the raucous bunch rushed out the door to redeem what few hours of twilight that remained before bed. Having played every game they could think of, Ray spoke up and said how about we play King of the Pier?"

$\sim$ 3 $\sim$

"HEALING
HOSPITALITY"

As he rushed through the doors not even giving them time to fully open, Thomas yelled out, "I'm Thomas Clayton, where is my son, Dairs?" The poor nurse at the desk, recoiled as if she'd been smacked right in the kisser. After composing herself and making a quick phone call, another nurse appeared and introduced herself. "No disrespect ma'am but I don't care if you're the Easter Bunny, I want to see my son, right now!" "Of course sir, but you can relax..." Cutting her off in mid-sentence, Mr. Clayton glared at her and said, "how can I relax when my son is in here somewhere fighting for his life?" "Well, you see that's the thing, Dairs is no longer fighting for his life, somehow the brain swelling has miraculously subsided and it looks like he is going to be just fine," said the nurse. "What was you name again?", he asked. The nurse smiled, "Hope, my name is Hope sir." Picking her up off the floor in a spin and giving her a genuine bear hug, Thomas beamed as he half spoke and half cried, "Well Hope, thank you, thank you, thank you. That's the best news I've heard all day." Composing herself after the unexpected "hug dance", Hope led the grateful parents to the room where Dairs lay resting with his faithful friend Dolian at his side, who had spent the evening of his eighteenth birthday in that hospital room praying for his injured friend. Quietly, the relieved father approached his son so as not to awaken him. As he reached the bedside he again fell to his knees in prayer, thanking God for answering his pleas. As he whispered "Amen" under his breath, Dairs eyes half opened and saw his Dad there as a tear slowly made its' way down his cheek. "Hey Dad, what happened, where am I?"

Elated, Thomas related the story to his son as best he could, with Dolian there filling in the gaps as the story unfolded. Overwhelmed by it all, the teenager laid his throbbing head back on the pillow and began to cry.

"MINDFUL OF A MIND FULL"

Having responded so well, and no longer in danger, Dairs was released from the hospital and allowed to go home. Winking at a pretty nurse on the way out, Dairs grinned from ear to ear as he stepped into the sunshine and hopped into the Chrysler New Yorker that was to be his chariot ride home. Though his head was still quite sore and the headache would last for weeks, Dairs was just grateful to be alive. The teen would spend the next few months in a state of contemplative thought, with so many things running up and down the staircase of his still aching brain. For several weeks, he would think of little else but how close he had come to death. He would often attempt to recall the events of that fateful day on the lake, but hard as he tried, nothing would come back. It was if an event in his own life had been locked up tight in a vault somewhere and he had not been entrusted with a key. It would be in the wake of the accident that he would grow ever closer to the Lord he had given his heart to 8 years earlier on May 5, 1977. "I'm just sixteen years old and I almost died," he would repeat to himself over and over. "Because of this episode, I am going to make every minute count, and be ready when it's my last! I am ALIVE therefore I am going to Live!", became his mantra.

He made good on that resolution for many years to come, saying yes to every opportunity that came his way no matter how crazy it seemed at the time, attempting to squeeze every drop out of life. Making friends everywhere he could, and experiencing anything that presented itself, carried him through adolescence and early adulthood with great joy, and lots of great stories. Ever mindful of his harrowing experience, it would be safe to say that Dairs had learned that nothing makes you feel more Alive than a brush with death itself.

~ 5 ~

"OUT OF FRIGHT OUT OF MIND"

Although Dairs would never completely forget the events from the Summer of '85, the memories began to fade like most memories do as weeks become months, that become years, that quickly become decades. The occurrence that had so shaped his young life had become more of a surreal story than reality, and the scare that once propelled him forward had dwindled. Other than being a story he rarely shared to encourage someone, the episode all but disappeared like snow on the ground as the

Spring sun comes to chase it away. Simply put, he was out of fright, so he put it out of mind.

In and of itself, forgetfulness is not inherently bad, but when it entails ignoring valuable life lessons taught through experience, it can be debilitating to the point of great destruction. Though intellectually Dairs knew this to be true, he like so many others, simply forgot. If that's where our story ended this could easily be deemed a tragedy, for it is tragic when wisdom is gained and lost, whether to forgetful complacency, or foolishness. Thankfully, this is NOT where the story ends - the best is yet to come.

~ 6 ~

"FORGET ME NOTS"

Though it is a certainty that time goes by at the "speed of life", and memories often fade, it is also a certainty that there are lessons to be learned every day we live. While some of these life lessons are strange and new, often the most vital lessons are gentle reminders of that which we already knew and need to recall for the journey ahead. The latter was the case for Dairs, the once hyperactive teen now three decades older, grown into a hyperactive husband to his beloved wife, Faith, father to his two crazy boys, Nolan and Michael, and friend to many the world over.

The voice on the phone was calm, yet pleading, "Hey Dairs, I wanted to let you know that Mom is quite sick and in the Intensive Care Unit at the hospital, could you go pray with her?" "Are you kidding, I love Mrs. B, I am on my way," came the immediate reply. Hopping into the truck he began to pray for this precious soul who had, taught him in Sunday School, mentored him throughout life and constantly told him, "you should always wear a white shirt, it just looks classy." At this he looked down and realized he was wearing what was likely to be the loudest red shirt he owned, "oh well, I don't have time to go home and change now, maybe she won't notice." Pulling into parking the lot, he threw in a breath strip and traipsed through the automatic doors into the unit. Being a small hospital, in a small town, where everyone knows everyone, (and most often are related) he saw the nurse pointing to Mrs. B's room before he could even ask. Entering the room quietly, Mrs. B smiled and waved him in. "How are you Mrs. B?" Always quick of wit the frail little lady smiled and responded, "I'm in the hospital, how do you think I am?" This was quickly followed with, "now that's quite the red shirt my boy!" Knowing he was busted he explained that he did not want to waste a single moment with her by going back to change into a white shirt. With what appeared to be a forgiving look she bid him sit beside her on the bed, and reached for his hand. Over the next few minutes, the two would share stories of their lives and experiences together with plenty of smiles throughout. Dairs could tell that his once outspoken friend was getting weaker by the moment as her voice trailed off mid-speech several times. Taking control of the conversation in an attempt to help her keep her strength up, Dairs begins to encourage Mrs. B, all the while careful not to sound condescending. "Young man, you are talking to me as if you think I am about to die, which I most certainly am not!" "Taken aback, he sheepishly said, "I am so sorry Mrs. B, I just know they said there is nothing else they can do for you..." Cutting him off the weary saint raised her voice authoritatively and squeezed his hand to the point that the inscription on his ring began to cut into his finger, "that's true, there ain't nothing else they can do for me, but I am not about to die, I am about to live because of what's already been done for me! You see my boy, most folks here think we are in the land of the living, headed to the land of the dead, but they've got it all wrong, I know that I am in the land of the dead and about to head to the land of the living!" You see, when Jesus died on that cross so long ago, and then rose out of that grave they put Him in, He killed death just as dead as a door-nail! I'm gonna' leave this old ball of dirt and head to heaven where He's got a placed fixed up just for me. That's just the way it is when you accept Jesus. You know yourself that the bible tells us we all have a reservation to die and there ain't no getting around it, and no changing it, and I know my reservation is almost here. Yes sir, I am about to walk through that valley of the shadow of death, but that shadow can't hurt me, I'm gonna' walk right by it onto the mountain of eternal life!" Dumbfounded by the strength and power with which this tiny little lady spoke, Dairs felt all the memories of that incident at the lake so many years ago flood over him like the waters that had covered him as he fell in that ill-fated day. The lessons that event had taught him came racing back in vivid color in his mind as if they had just happened all over again. Realizing this moment was not supposed to be about him, he was jarred back to the situation at hand, and smiled at Mrs. B and said, "you are so very right Mrs. B, so very right, and isn't it wonderful to have such hope that whether we are here or there we are very much ALIVE?" Feeling confident she was doing much better after her powerful outburst, Dairs sat for a few moments more making small talk, when Mrs. B raised her head and squeezed his already sore hand once more and said, "That's enough talk sonny, say a prayer for me it's time for me to get on home." Not fully comprehending what she was trying to get across, Dairs bowed his head and obliged his charge with a heartfelt prayer. Raising his head and saying, "Amen", Dairs watched as the look on her face became as peaceful as a child asleep in their father's arms. The little fireball of a lady who had just rekindled long forgotten emotions and resolve from his childhood by way of her forceful discourse breathed one last breath and in her own words became **ALIVE**.

Don't let a brush with death be what it takes for you to realize you are ALIVE and may you have the calm assurance that when death does come to visit, you are ready to be more ALIVE than ever before.

Happy Easter!

Romans 6:5

M-T

POEMS OF THE SEASON

SONRISE

On a hill far away,
On an Old Rugged Cross,
Hung my sin, my shame ...
My hurt and my loss,

It was there on that Cross,
My Savior did die,
To conquer my death,
In His blood my hope lies,

As He breathed His last,
The sun escaped sight,
As the Savior proved,
He was the world's true light.

Low in a grave they placed Him that day,
But that grave could not hold Him,
The Stone rolled away.

Three days soon passed and the Son rose
again,
Now all who believe can live beyond sin.

Though Death will soon visit,
With our appointment to die,
Because of the SONrise,
The believer is forever ALIVE!

DDC 2021

THE ANSWER

Distressed, lonely, weary or worn,
The answer to all in a stable was born.
Depressed, anguished, bitter or frayed,
In the manger the solution was laid,
Troubled, searching, hopelessly lost,
One loved you enough to pay the great-
est cost,
Consumed by your lust for Earth's entic-
ing greed,
One died on a cross to fill your greatest
need.
When all else leaves you empty and seek-
ing in vain,
Just turn your eyes to Jesus and call on
His name.
There is no friend more faithful,
No treasure more dear,
Than the peace of eternally knowing,
There's nothing left to fear.

DDC 2017

FAKE NEWS

The day will come when life is done,
I'll cross to the other side,
And when it does they'll surely say this
man has finally died,
But don't believe if this you hear,
For not a word is truth,
An empty tomb says He still lives,
Which means that I can too,
My death was killed by
Jesus Christ so many years ago,
So when I leave this earthly home ,
I've a better place to go,
So when I'm done do not be sad,
I have not truly died,
Let joy take hold and smile for me,
I've never been more alive.

DDC 2020

THE REAL STORY

Mark 15 - 16

15 And straightway in the morning the chief priests held a consultation with the elders and scribes and the whole council, and bound Jesus, and carried him away, and delivered him to Pilate.[2] And Pilate asked him, Art thou the King of the Jews? And he answering said unto them, Thou sayest it.[3] And the chief priests accused him of many things: but he answered nothing.[4] And Pilate asked him again, saying, Answerest thou nothing? behold how many things they witness against thee.[5] But Jesus yet answered nothing; so that Pilate marvelled.[6] Now at that feast he released unto them one prisoner, whomsoever they desired.[7] And there was one named Barabbas, which lay bound with them that had made insurrection with him, who had committed murder in the insurrection. [8] And the multitude crying aloud began to desire him to do as he had ever done unto them. [9] But Pilate answered them, saying, Will ye that I release unto you the King of the Jews? [10] For he knew that the chief priests had delivered him for envy. [11] But the chief priests moved the people, that he should rather release Barabbas unto them. [12] And Pilate answered and said again unto them, What will ye then that I shall do unto him whom ye call the King of the Jews? [13] And they cried out again, Crucify him. [14] Then Pilate said unto them, Why, what evil hath he done? And they cried out the more exceedingly, Crucify him. [15] And so Pilate, willing to content the people, released Barabbas unto them, and delivered Jesus, when he had scourged him, to be crucified. [16] And the soldiers led him away into the hall, called Praetorium; and they call together the whole band. [17] And they clothed him with purple, and platted a crown of thorns, and put it about his head, [18] And began to salute him, Hail, King of the Jews! [19] And they smote him on the head with a reed, and did spit upon him, and bowing their knees worshipped him. [20] And when they had mocked him, they took off the purple from him, and put his own clothes on him, and led him out to crucify him. [21] And they compel one Simon a Cyrenian, who passed by, coming out of the country, the father of Alexander and Rufus, to bear his cross. [22] And they bring him unto the place Golgotha, which is, being interpreted, The place of a skull. [23] And they gave him to drink wine mingled with myrrh: but he received it not. [24] And when they had crucified him, they parted his garments, casting lots upon them, what every man should take. [25] And it was the third hour, and they crucified him. [26] And the superscription of his accusation was written over, The King Of The Jews. [27] And with him they crucify two thieves; the one on his right hand, and the other on his left. [28] And the scripture was fulfilled, which saith, And he was numbered with the transgressors. [29] And they that passed by railed on him, wagging their heads, and saying, Ah, thou that destroyest the temple, and buildest it in three days, [30] Save thyself, and come down from the cross.[31] Likewise also the chief priests mocking said among themselves with the scribes, He saved others; himself he cannot save.[32] Let Christ the King of Israel descend now from the cross, that we may see and believe. And they that were crucified with him reviled him.[33] And when the sixth hour was come, there was darkness over the whole land until the ninth hour.[34] And at the ninth hour Jesus cried with a loud voice, saying, Eloi, Eloi, lama sabachthani? which is, being interpreted, My God, my God, why hast thou forsaken me?[35] And some of them that stood by, when they heard it, said, Behold, he calleth Elias.[36] And one ran and filled a spunge full of vinegar, and put it on a reed, and gave him to drink, saying, Let alone; let us see whether Elias will come to take him down.[37] And Jesus cried with a loud voice, and gave up the ghost.[38] And the veil of the temple was rent in twain from the top to the bottom.[39] And when the centurion, which stood over against him, saw that he so cried out, and gave up the ghost, he said, Truly this man was the Son of God.[40] There were also women looking on afar off: among whom was Mary Magdalene, and Mary the mother of James the less and of Joses, and Salome;[41] (Who also, when he was in Galilee, followed him, and ministered unto him;) and many other women which came up with him unto Jerusalem.[42] And now when the even was come, because it was the preparation, that is, the day before the sabbath,[43] Joseph of Arimathaea, an honourable counsellor, which also waited for the kingdom of God, came, and went in boldly unto Pilate, and craved the body of Jesus.[44] And Pilate marvelled if he were already dead: and calling unto him the centurion, he asked him whether he had been any while dead.[45] And when he knew it of the centurion, he gave the body to Joseph.[46] And he bought fine linen, and took him down, and wrapped him in the linen, and laid him in a sepulchre which was hewn out of a rock, and rolled a stone unto the door of the sepulchre.[47] And Mary Magdalene and Mary the mother of Joses beheld where he was laid.**16** And when the sabbath was past, Mary Magdalene, and Mary the mother of James, and Salome, had bought sweet spices, that they might come and anoint him. [2] And very early in the morning the first day of the week, they came unto the sepulchre at the rising of the sun. [3] And they said among themselves, Who shall roll us away the stone from the door of the sepulchre? [4] And when they looked, they saw that the stone was rolled away: for it was very great. [5] And entering into the sepulchre, they saw a young man sitting on the right side, clothed in a long white garment; and they were affrighted. [6] And he saith unto them, Be not affrighted: Ye seek Jesus of Nazareth, which was crucified: he is risen; he is not here: behold the place where they laid him.

The Beginning